Pebble Plus

BIRDS OF PREY

Turkey VULTURES

by Mary R. Dunn

Consulting Editor: Gail Saunders-Smith, PhD

Consultant: Jessica Ehrgott, Bird and Mammal
Trainer, Downtown Aquarium, Denver

CAPSTONE PRESS
a capstone imprint

Pebble Plus is published by Capstone Press,
1710 Roe Crest Drive, North Mankato, Minnesota 56003
www.capstonepub.com

Library of Congress Cataloging-in-Publication Data
Dunn, Mary R.
Turkey Vultures / by Mary R. Dunn.
pages cm.
Includes bibliographical references and index.
Summary: "Describes the characteristics, habitat, behavior, life cycle, and
threats to turkey vultures"—Provided by publisher.
Audience: Ages 5 to 8.
Audience: Grades K to 3.
ISBN 978-1-4914-2094-2 (library binding)
ISBN 978-1-4914-2312-7 (pbk.)
ISBN 978-1-4914-2335-6 (ebook pdf)
1. Turkey vulture—Juvenile literature. I. Title.
QL696.C53D865 2014
598.9'2—dc23   2014032784

Editorial Credits
Jeni Wittrock, editor; Peggie Carley and Janet Kusmierski, designers;
Svetlana Zhurkin, media researcher; Katy LaVigne, production specialist

Photo Credits
Alamy: Christopher Price, 15; iStockphotos: erniedecker, 17; Minden Pictures:
Stephen Dalton, 21; Shutterstock: Arend Trent, 7, balounm, back cover
(background), Domenic Gareri, 5, Gary C. Tognoni, cover, back cover, 19,
Jan-Dirk Hansen, 11, Jay Ondreicka, 9, Paul S. Wolf, 13, Tony Campbell, 1

Note to Parents and Teachers

The Birds of Prey set supports national science standards related
to life science. This book describes and illustrates turkey vultures.
The images support early readers in understanding the text. The
repetition of words and phrases helps early readers learn new
words. This book also introduces early readers to subject-specific
vocabulary words, which are defined in the Glossary section. Early
readers may need assistance to read some words and to use the
Table of Contents, Glossary, Read More, Internet Sites, Critical
Thinking Using the Common Core, and Index sections of the book.

Printed in the United States of America in Stevens Point, Wisconsin
102014   008479WZS15

Table of Contents

Garbage Gobblers

Turkey vultures circle the skies looking for food. When night falls, they rest in trees with their families.

Up Close!

Turkey vultures look like turkeys. They have brown-black feathers and bald, red heads. Their bills and feet are white.

Turkey vultures have long but light bodies. They weigh about 5 pounds (2 kilograms). Their wings stretch almost 6 feet (1.8 meters) wide.

Six kinds of turkey vultures
live around the world.
They make their homes near
open land with few trees.

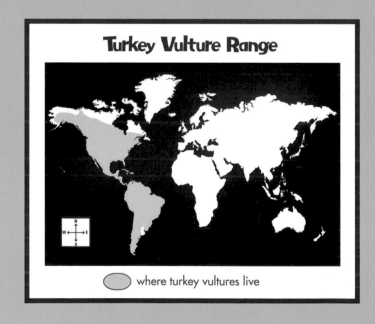

Turkey Vulture Range

where turkey vultures live

Mealtime

Turkey vultures don't hunt
live prey. These scavengers eat
animals that are already dead.
The stinky smell leads vultures
to their next meal.

Growing Up

Female turkey vultures find

a safe place to lay their eggs.

But these birds don't build nests.

In about 40 days, one or two

fuzzy chicks hatch.

Both parents care for the chicks and feed them. In 70 days the chicks can fly. Adults form groups called roosts. Turkey vultures live about 20 years.

Keeping Safe

Owls and raccoons eat turkey vulture eggs and chicks. Angry turkey vultures vomit rotten food at predators. The smell makes predators go away.

The number of turkey vultures is growing. Laws help protect these amazing scavengers. Helpful turkey vultures keep Earth clean.

Glossary

bald—bare skin with no hair, fur, or feathers

chick—a young bird

predator—an animal that hunts other animals for food

prey—an animal hunted by other animals for food

roost—a group of turkey vultures

scavenger—an animal that feeds on animals that are already dead

vomit—to throw up food or liquid from the stomach through the mouth

Read More

Arnosky, Jim. *Thunder Birds: Nature's Flying Predators.* New York: Sterling Children's Books, 2011.

Dunn, Mary. *California Condors.* Birds of Prey. North Mankato, Minn.: Capstone Press, 2015.

Kalman, Bobbie. *Nature's Cleaners.* Big Science Ideas. New York: Crabtree Pub., 2009.

Internet Sites

FactHound offers a safe, fun way to find Internet sites related to this book. All of the sites on FactHound have been researched by our staff.

Here's all you do:

Visit *www.facthound.com*

Type in this code: 9781491420942

Super-cool stuff! Check out projects, games and lots more at **www.capstonekids.com**

Critical Thinking Using the Common Core

How do turkey vultures find food?
(Key Ideas and Details)

Why would having a light body be helpful to a turkey vulture?
(Integration of Knowledge and Ideas)

Index

Word Count: 198
Grade: 1
Early-Intervention Level: 14